# Was I Born in The Right Family?

**GRENITA HALL**

# TABLE OF CONTENT

| | |
|---|---|
| INTRODUCTION | V |
| CHAPTER 1: GRANDMA'S HOUSE | 1 |
| CHAPTER 2: THERE HAS TO BE A BETTER LIFE | 21 |
| CHAPTER 3: HERE TODAY, GONE TOMORROW | 41 |
| CHAPTER 4: WHO AM I? | 57 |

# DEDICATION

This book is dedicated to my mother, Willie Mae Smith. I love and miss you dearly. May you rest in the hands of God.

I also dedicate this book to my husband, Herbert Hall, my sons, and daughters. Thank you for all your support. To all those that encouraged me to move forward, I am grateful for you as well.

God's blessings to you all.

# TABLE OF CONTENT

| | |
|---|---|
| INTRODUCTION | V |
| CHAPTER 1: GRANDMA'S HOUSE | 1 |
| CHAPTER 2: THERE HAS TO BE A BETTER LIFE | 21 |
| CHAPTER 3: HERE TODAY, GONE TOMORROW | 41 |
| CHAPTER 4: WHO AM I? | 54 |

# INTRODUCTION

This book is based on a true story, but the names of the people were changed for privacy reasons. I am telling my story now because when the Lord placed it in my heart to do so, I was afraid for many years. Shame got in the way, and I was embarrassed to let people know the truth about my life. I was scared of what they might have thought about my little sister and me. I did not want people to look at us differently or maybe treat us differently. There were times when I would share bits and pieces of my life, but not a lot. Many would tell me to write my story, but I would turn the other way. Later, I realized telling just a little of my life could not heal me because there were more than bits and pieces in me to tell. God has given me the love and strength to say it all, so I no longer worry about how other's might feel about my little sister or me.

My story was written to give others the courage to tell their story. Even if you are not a writer, write it down. If you don't know how, pray, and God will show you a way to tell it. God will open the door for you to have all you need. No more being scared or afraid. Release your fears, and the doors shall open. The weight of the world will fall off your shoulders once you complete your assignment of telling your testimony. It might sound crazy, but it's ok to forgive those that hurt you. I mean, really hurt you! Love them despite it all because forgiveness is not for the person or persons. It's for you. You will be free from anger and pain. Your mind will be at ease and your heart pure. Forgive so you will be able to smile again.

Know that you are wonderfully made by the hands of God. I send blessings to all that read my book. I pray you release your story today because it can be someone else's healing. I am now healed from all hurt and pain of my past, simply because I forgave and released my story. I smile even when life throws me new curveballs. I'm so free, and I am finally living. Are you ready to live?

# CHAPTER 1
## Grandma's House

My name is Grenita Smith-Hall. I'm now fifty-two years old writing this book. I have so much to share about my childhood because I went through a lot. I was born in West Philadelphia. My mother is Willie Mae Smith, and my father is Eddie Folks. I have two brothers and three sisters. We were raised by my mother's mother, Mrs. Mollie Smith. My mother and her family were born and raised down south, Lake City, South Carolina, to be exact. My grandma played basketball there and was great at what she did. She was a dark skin, slim-built woman who stood about six foot nine inches. My grandma had pretty silky flowing black hair. Her eyes were tiny and beady, and she spoke with a deep voice. My aunts would share her stories with us growing up. They would brag about their mother's accomplishments, which was ok with me because as kids, I knew not to say anything, whether it was good or bad. My grandma had two sons, Alfonso and Willie. She also had her five daughters, Emma,

Laney, Willie Mae, Mary, and Glenda. They moved from Lake City, South Carolina, to West Philadelphia on the forty-six hundred block of Brown Street. That is where my mother met my dad. I am the middle girl out of five children.

My mom and dad split and my mom could not raise any of us, so my grandma stepped up. My mom battled with demons, and it eventually consumed her. My baby sister and I never had the chance to see her after my grandma took over. It's crazy because my other siblings had the opportunity to spend time with our mom. Everyone even knew where she lived, except me and my baby sister, Scholar. We were told that no one knew where she was as a child, but we knew it was all lies. I thought it was strange for them to lie to us. What was the reason for it all?

I still wonder why my grandma wanted to raise all five of us. I guess I'll never know. I don't remember anything about where I was born. I remember a lot about 948 North Fifty Street. I was around six or seven. We lived there for years; my grandma owned that house, so everyone was comfortable. There was no hurry to move. The neighbors on the block knew her and did things for one another. It was like having one big family. Sometimes it was hard to remember names, and you dared not do anything wrong. They watched you like a hawk and would whip you as well but would be friendly now and then.

Grandma Mollie wasn't such a pleasant person; she was always mad at Scholar and me. Trying our best to please her, we would do anything for her. She already had us doing everything as it was, so we eventually ran out of new ideas. There was nothing extra to do to please her. I remember one summer; I was no more than six years old. Grandma Mollie woke scholar and me up; we were so tired. Trying to get our balance, she was yelling, "Get up, get up! Get the broom Peanut and Scholar. Scholar, you get the bucket and put some warm water and pine oil in it, just a little bit. Peanut, when you are done sweeping, start mopping."

Now I didn't understand this; there were other kids in the house beside us, but she never woke them up. I knew it had to be around six a.m. in the morning because I could hear the birds chirping. We were moving slowly because we were still half-sleep. We wondered why our grandma was the evil lady that only had us around to work. Scholar and I couldn't believe it. She was always nasty to us, and she didn't hide it at all. I felt sorry for Scholar; she was a year younger than me. Grandma would raise her voice to Scholar, "Hurry up! You don't have all day. Move faster than that before I knock the black off you." That seemed to be her favorite words. She would use them all the time. Knowing her, if we didn't move fast, we would find our teeth on the floor. So, we moved as fast as we could. We never looked up. We just cleaned and did whatever was needed as quickly as possible. Later in the morning, when we were done sweeping and mopping, we both went back to our room to lie down. Grandma Mollie would stand in the living room, and she would yell, "Where ya'll slick behinds think you going?" "Back to our rooms," we replied. "No, you are not! When I'm up, you are up," grandma said. I then said to grandma, "Would you like me to wake up the other kids?" That made her so angry that she slapped spit from my mouth. My lip began bleeding, just a little. I said nothing afterward. Being afraid, Scholar said, "Grandma, what else do you want me to clean?" Grandma turned and said, "The both of you get some rags and put some fresh water in a bucket with a little pine oil and wash down the wood around the walls."

That was truly insane because there are enough kids in the house for all of us to get chores done in a few hours. I never understood why this lady had it out for the two of us. I would talk to God about it on the regular, hoping to get a response. I wanted to know why. I would see Grandma Mollie pray, so I figured, why not try it myself. Maybe God could move us from this hateful woman's house. Scholar and I didn't believe we were in the right family because of the harsh treatment. Maybe God made a mistake and just didn't realize it is what I thought for so long. I would cry out every day, "Please Lord, help us. We need you right now."

That didn't go so well because time moved on and we were growing up still stuck where we were. It's sad to say our childhood was not days of sweet memories. Scholar and I never got the chance to be kids; we were always doing grown-up things. We were washing clothes, cooking for the house, running errands, etc. I never learned to jump rope, play hopscotch or red-light green light, or ride a bike. I felt we were only put on the earth to be punished for what our mother might have done. I mean, what else could it have been? Was it really about the color of our skin?

I wonder, "Was my family prejudiced against their kind?" Scholar was nine years old, and I was ten. We were stair steps in age which implied my mother had us back-to-back. It didn't matter to me because we never knew her anyway, so I didn't feel I missed anything. My siblings and I were all together, so I didn't feel alone. I just hated the fact that maybe my mother didn't love us. These thoughts were constantly rolling in my mind. There was a story of my mother from different family members that she went through hell and couldn't take it anymore. So, I thought, "Why she kept having babies for your mother to take and treat three good and two bad?" I would wonder how she looked. Was she ugly or beautiful? We were told by our family a lot we weren't good-looking kids. "Maybe that's why Scholar and I were mistreated," I thought.

Or maybe they were just ugly inside and out and took it out on us. When grandma and Aunt Mary got drunk, horrible looking wasn't good enough for them. Liquor made them do crazy things, even to my little sister and me. The worst came out of them then, and the sad thing is I don't ever recall them saying "I love you," even on a sober day. When I look back, none of them said it to each other, so I guess I was asking for too much. Maybe none of them knew what love was, nor did they love themselves. As time went on, nothing got better for Scholar and me. It always seemed to worsen for us two, but not for my oldest brother Robert and sister. Even our baby brother got treated better than us. Grandma Mollie would look at me sometimes and say, "What the hell are you looking at with your little light self? You and your black sister?" The way I felt inside was, "Who would help us out of this terror?" That was making no sense at all to me. Then, Aunt Mary was worse than grandma. She and Grandma

Mollie were two peas in a pot, always scheming and up to no good. We were kids, but not dumb! We saw things you wouldn't believe involving both of them. They were just two evil people. I would pray that the Lord changed them both to be good, but I'm guessing you have to want it for God to do it.

Maybe we were just in the wrong family. That's what I felt between the pulling of our hair and saying harsh things like, "You some ugly girls! No man is going ever to want any one of you." It hurt, but we didn't care about a man wanting us because we were just kids. Grandma would always say, "Just like your mother" after each insult. Then Aunt Mary would continually say, "Yea, y'all are nasty and filthy looking. You are going to have babies with different men just like your mammy." Aunt Mary would then say, "Don't look at me!" We were always scared, so we looked down to the floor. I was deeply hurt so much inside for too long. I would cry out, "God help us, please," when we could smell the liquor on her breath a mile away. We knew it was another level of terror in store for us.

I remember when Scholar and I would be in our room playing with our dolls that was so cheaply made. They were the reject dolls from the dollar store that was so skinny and had rough hair. The dolls would break all the time. The arms and legs would fall off easily. We would just put them back on and laugh. My oldest sister got good dolls like baby alive and Barbie. She even got an Easy Bake Oven set! She was treated like a queen. We were not jealous at all. Scholar and I just wanted Grandma Mollie to love us too. That's what we hoped and prayed for each day.

Sometimes we pretend our dolls were Aunt Mary and Grandma Mollie, even though the dolls were white. We would mock them and didn't care. Thank God they never heard us! Grandma probably would have beaten the blood out of us. We needed something to keep us occupied because when the other kids were outside, we weren't allowed to go out and play. When grandma decided to watch television, we had to go upstairs because we were not allowed to watch. Grandma had one of those big pretty floor model televisions that were in color. Scholar and I never asked to come downstairs to watch with them. We knew that was like asking for a free whooping. We hated the summer because we never got a chance to do anything other than clean and stay in the room. We had more fun in school when other kids did not pick on us.

Aunt Mary spoke to my grandma about putting Scholar in a special class, expressing she was slow. There wasn't anything slow about Scholar, though. Aunt Mary told grandma she could get an SSI check for her. They both were greedy for a dollar. Well, it worked out in Aunt Mary's favor because she had Scholar put in a special learning class, and the checks began rolling. Mary even went a step further and said Peanut needs to be in one too, but it didn't work in their favor concerning me. I showed my teacher that I was smart. Scholar could have demonstrated to her teacher that she was brilliant too, but I believe she didn't think she was at the time after all the negative words they fed to her. Being fearful is a tricky thing, and it can have you feeling like life doesn't matter. I would feel this way often with certain situations in my life. I always prayed that God would show me a way out of all the hell and turmoil in my family. I thought they would be loving and kind, but that was far from their character.

We didn't ask to be born nor to live with this family. We would earnestly pray to be placed in the family that God had for us. The nights and days always seemed so long. Where was our help? Some days I felt like my strength had all gone. Two little girls that did no wrong to anyone had to endure torment for so many years. Those in my family knew what was going on, but nobody wanted to step up. Two relatives tried to help, but they could only do so much. They had their own lives to live, so Scholar and I held on to each other. At the time of it all, we were all we had. We were hoping and praying that God cared and loved us enough to get us away from this family fast! I thought we were going to die at times because we were abuse and depressed as a result. I felt our superhero got lost along the way, so there was no one to free us. Where was our savior? I refused to settle for the abuse.

I did not accept any of my family members calling me dumb either. They said it often to hurt our feelings, but I knew it wasn't true. I did not want the kids in school laughing at me or teasing me because I was in a slower learning class. That would have been too embarrassing, and I indeed would not have had peace in school. The school was the only place I felt safe despite getting picked on for other reasons. We had some friends in school, but we were not popular. The outcast people connected with us because they got picked on too. I guess we were ok hanging with them, or it would have just been Scholar and me. We were less fortunate and could not wear the finest things, but we learned to accept that. We did not complain about it. One would have thought that grandma was poor because she lived modestly and did not do much shopping. She knew how to save money. She was far from poor, all the money she would collect for us. Grandma was just mean!

Back in the seventies, people on our block had their kid's looking beautiful and well put together. My oldest brother and sister looked lovely all the time. Scholar and I wore secondhand clothes. Either people gave us their clothes, or our grandma went to the thrift store. The clothes didn't always fit, but what were we to say? We had to wear them, or we would've gotten the blood beaten out of us.

If we were not cleaning or in school, we stayed in our room. We would have girl talk, make up games to place, and sing low. We wouldn't want anyone to hear us. Even our oldest brother and sister would turn against us. They were royalty in grandma's eyes. I never understood why, but at times I felt my Grandma Mollie was "colored stroked." That's what the old folks would say about white folks down south. They would value the light-skinned people more than the dark-skinned people. Down south, they would look at your skin color to judge you before anything else. My sister, Claudine, was darker than Scholar and me, while my brother Robert was as light as me. So, I was not too sure if grandma was playing the color card with us. I do know she always referred to our skin color when she would curse us out.

Grandma Mollie kept food in the house. We did not go without, but she would purposely give Scholar and me a little food on our plates for each meal. She made it clear that was all we were going to get. We better not had asked for a second plate to eat because grandma was not having that. We just went to our room after we were done. Grandma knew how to cook well. She would put other cooks to shame if there was a competition.

Grandma would get up and start breakfast around 5:30 in the morning. Scholar and I could smell the delicious fatback aroma in the air. Some called it salted pork. I also remember her creamy grits with butter, and she made the best biscuits! They were to die for because they were so good! I would sit up sometimes and lick my lips, imaging that taste of breakfast already in my mouth. She would call us downstairs around eight in the morning after preparing the table. Grandma would yell, "Come on down and eat! Don't come down until you wash your face and brush your teeth!" We hurried up and gathered at the table to say grace, giving thanks to God for the food before we ate. Grandma would always conclude grace. After she was finally done, we would all start to eat.

Eating at the table with everyone was not always a smooth task. Our sister, Claudine, would start teasing Scholar, calling her names. She would say things like, "You so black! Now say something, and I'm going to tell everyone to look at your hair." She was so mean at times. That was sad because we are sisters, but Claudine only said and did what Grandma Mollie would say and do to us. It bothered Scholar a lot; therefore, it bothered me too. Grandma would always rush Scholar and me to eat and leave the table. She would say, "Scholar and Peanut, hurry up! You both should have been done by now!" The food was so good and very small in portion, so we tried to make it last. It was nowhere near a full plate when it was served to us, so we had to imagine that it was enough. To avoid getting in further trouble and yelled at some more, we hurried up and finished our food. There were times grandma would snatch our plates before we were done and start slapping us in the face because she felt we were taking too long to eat. It was crazy! I hated every minute of the abuse. Scholar and I had to go through this regularly.

It was unbelievable at times what we had to endure. I couldn't wrap my mind around everything that had happened. Every day we ate like it was our last day on earth because life was so unpredictable for us. That was how grandma had us feeling all the time. We were afraid of her, and I knew she didn't love us. She just went through the motions with us because we were family. She never cared about us and could not wait to torment us every day. I wished I belonged to another family! I would daydream about my new family all the time. I would never make out their faces, but I knew they had smiles towards Scholar and me.

After breakfast, grandma would have Scholar, and I cleaned the kitchen. Grandma Mollie would say, "Peanut, wash the dishes, and Scholar, sweep the floor. Don't touch my pots. I'll put the rest of my food away." I knew she was lying to us about the amount of food she cooked. There was always so much food left to put up in the refrigerator. Scholar and I could've gotten a second plate or even a full plate, to begin with, but I guess she did not want us to have the food.

After we were done cleaning the kitchen, we would go back upstairs and sit down. What else were we going to do? We couldn't play outside with the other kids, not even with our siblings. Grandma Mollie wouldn't let us look at television either. That was indeed the house of horror, and I was over it all. Aunt Mary never wanted to eat but would take some of grandma's food to feed her dog. The dog ate better than us at times. Aunt Mary was always drinking liquor and never had room for food. Aunt Mary would always drunk playing with that dog in the living room. She named him Duke. The dog would jump on the furniture, and grandma would not say anything about it, but she did not even allow us to sit in the living room. We better not had thought about it either because she would try to knock our heads off our shoulders!

There were times Aunt Mary would call Scholar and me back downstairs and make us stand in the middle of the floor so she could laugh at us. "You both are some ugly kids," Aunt Mary would say. She would then call Claudine and Robert into the living room and say, "I want you all to fight. The winner gets fifty cents." Well, back then, fifty-cent was a lot of money for children. Claudine and Robert did not even need the money because Grandma Mollie would give them money all the time. Scholar and I would never get any money, so we thought this was our chance to get some finally. Not that we wanted to fight our siblings for it, but we were damned if we did and damned if we didn't. They would have beaten us up anyway. Of course, Scholar and I lost each time. They were bigger than us! The odds were always stacked against us. They would always win the fight no matter how hard we fought back. Aunt Mary would provoke this madness every time she was drinking at the house. We were her entertainment for the day. They would get the fifty-cent each while we had to go to our room beat up and exhausted.

Aunt Mary would send our siblings to Mrs. Green's store to get brown paper bags full of cookies and candy of different flavors. She would tease us with the snacks she had. She would always hold her hand out to us and ask, "You want some?" We would say, "Yea." Then our sister, Claudine, would joke with us and say, "Sike your mic! You can't have any!" They would laugh at us and walk away, giving us none. Claudine could be mean at times. I don't know why we fell for that trick each time anyway. We knew in our hearts that Claudine, Robert, or Aunt Mary wasn't giving up that juicy candy or snack. We would stay in our room at times to not have to deal with the abuse. Scholar and I would play make-believe to imagine we were in a better place because reality was too hard at times. That seemed to be the time we were at peace. We would dream of being princesses in a castle where we made up all the rules and had fun all the time. We imagined our castle having a sweet smell of cinnamon and brown sugar in the atmosphere. I don't know why, but those two fragrances together made us feel at home. Our castle was trimmed with gold and had yellow and red roses planted all around the outside garden. We even had a password to get into the castle, which was "Love." We would eat sugar donuts, sweet honey buns and drink hot chocolate for each meal in our castle. There would be only sunshine outside and no rain. The rain made the days gloomy because we would think back on the hateful things our family did to us. Therefore, sunny days made us feel free from the wickedness of our relatives. As we played pretend, we would close our eyes, never wanting to open them to the reality of our lives again. We would smile and laugh as our eyes were closed. As long as no one called us downstairs, we felt safe and free.

We would even say things to ourselves to build up our self-esteem. Our family tore us down enough in one day to last us a lifetime, so we figured it was time to build ourselves up. "I'm a beautiful queen with lots of money. I wear fancy clothes and drive a fancy car to get away whenever I want," I would say to myself and Scholar. Scholar would say, "I'm a queen too, Peanut, just like you! I will one day treat my kids like royalty as well. People are going to work for us." I would believe in my heart for this all to be true only to open my eyes to what was the truth at that moment in time. After pretending was over, we would look out the window to watch the kids play on the back streets, having fun. We hoped one day to be the kids having fun and enjoying ourselves outside. I guess it didn't hurt to have hope.

I remember Aunt Emma visiting us, and she would try her best to help us whenever she could. Everyone was afraid of Grandma Mollie for some reason, so they did not want to get involved or on her bad side. Aunt Emma worked a lot and spent the remainder of her time with her man, Mr. Joe. He was pleasant and worked for Septa Transportation. We did not know too much more about Mr. Joe other than he would buy liquor from grandma sometimes. Me. Joe wasn't like Aunt Mary when he would drink, so that was a plus. Grandma's side hustle was selling liquor for cheap, and after hours, many people visited her for business exchanges. I guess Aunt Emma did not want to mess it up for Mr. Joe, so she did not cross the line with grandma.

Scholar and I got older, but nothing got better. Each birthday would roll around, and we never had a party, cake, ice cream, or acknowledgment at all. A few family members barely wanted to say happy birthday. We ate dinner, as usual, cleaned the kitchen, and went to bed. It was just another regular day. Grandma Mollie tried being friendly for a little, but that didn't last long because that was not her heart.

Friday nights at grandma's house were the time she sold dinners to the neighborhood. She would usually sell fried chicken, fish, fresh greens, string beans, potatoes, macaroni & cheese, salad, beer, and liquor. Grandma had a box of overflowing beer that she would take outside and pump three times, signaling that it was party time! The stench of cigarettes had the house smelling so bad. Her friends and family came left and right to join in on the party. She was selling dinners, but it always turned out to be a house party. She always thought we were dumb and had no idea of what was going on in the house. Grandma would check on us upstairs to make sure we all were in bed after she fed us early. She did not want us in the way or grown folks' faces. Grandma would say, "Nobody better get out the bed!" Claudine would sarcastically ask, "Well, what if we have to go to the bathroom?" Grandma Mollie replied, "Go to the bathroom and get your butts back in the bed! Don't play with me either!" We knew she meant business, so we stayed out of her way.

When grandma went back downstairs to entertaining

her company, Claudine would always ask us if we wanted to peek downstairs. We would be nervous, but curious so we would go with her. Claudine would say she wouldn't tell on us even though it was her plan. To peek downstairs, we crawled on our stomachs like rattlesnakes down the cold hard wooden floor. Then slid down the hard stairs as quietly as we could, looking and breathing hard. We were all scared at the same time. I don't know why Scholar and I decided to listen to Claudine and Robert. They weren't to be trusted at all. They would roll over on a dead man if they had to just to get out of trouble.

We all had our heads sticking through the banister polls just looking at all the old folks' party as if they had no care in the world. Or maybe partying was their world, and that was the only time they came alive. We just prayed that we would not get caught out of the bed. After we finally went back to bed, I was surprised Claudine and Robert never said a word about what we had all did that night. I guess they knew they would get a whipping, too, for not listening to grandma. That was Friday nights at grandma's house. What I learned was that grown folks knew how to party hard.

Another memory I cannot forget is Miss Trudy, and Miss Jones would chew and spit tobacco all night long. It was so gross to watch them chew it as if it was gum. I remember Miss Jones was the Number lady. Grandma Mollie would write out her numbers and ask us to take them across the street to Miss Jones and yell at us not to drop the paper. Grandma put the paper with the numbers on it and some money in a brown paper bag for Miss Jones. It was usually a bunch of pennies. You could win big with just pennies back then. Grandma and Miss Jones made a lot of money playing numbers.

Gambling the way grandma and Miss Jones did was illegal. The whole neighborhood knew Miss Jones ran the numbers, and for a while, it was kept secret from the authorities. One day I guess someone did not have it anymore, and they called the police. I remember the cops pulling up on the block in the black and white police cars as if they had been surveilling the gambling for some time already. The cops knew exactly where to go to pick up Miss Jones. Miss Jones tried to hide the written numbers in the chicken butt she was preparing for dinner, but that didn't work out too well for her. She was busted and told my grandma she wasn't taking the rap for her because she got caught there as well. Grandma was so upset at Miss Jones. The police took them, and grandma had to stay a day in jail. That made my day. Scholar and I were so happy we did not know what to do with ourselves. Aunt Mary had to get some money together for the police to release grandma that next day, or she would have been there longer. Aunt Emma stayed at the house to watch us until grandma came home.

Well, at least I can say God answered our prayers for that day. When grandma came home from jail, she was fussing. The first two people grandma called downstairs were Scholar and me. She wanted us to clean up the living room and dining room. Aunt Emma stepped in to try and save us, suggesting that grandma needed to allow us to eat first then clean afterward. Grandma told her she wanted the house cleaned in a hurry no matter if we ate or not. We were the maids of the house for everyone. Grandma Mollie was mad about everything that day, but when she started counting the money from the dinners she sold, she began to smile. She put the money down her bra and went out to the porch. Grandma wanted to find out who called the cops on Miss Jones, but she never did because nobody spoke up or knew who it was.

After Scholar and I were done cleaning, we informed grandma. She said with a nasty voice, "Go eat some cereal and get back upstairs!" Everyone else got a hot-cooked meal, but we had to eat cereal because everything was stored away when we were done cleaning. We obeyed and tried not to feel sad. Grandma Mollie made it known that she didn't care about the two of us at all. She made it seem like the world was better off without us, and we had no place value. We always felt useless, and I would ask God, "What is my place in this life?" I was just eleven years old. "Why was I born?" I thought daily. It was hard being alive when your place in life is unknown, and you don't understand who you are. We had not one clue, and it bothered me every day. We would shut our bedroom door to feel a little more secure in the house.

Grandma would notice and say, "Open my door! Ya'll don't pay rent. Neither of you has a pot to piss in or a window to throw it out!" Scholar and I would laugh to ourselves and say under our breath, "Oh, yes, we do!" We thought to ourselves that we could throw it out her window after peeing in her pot. Or maybe stick it under her bed. We would laugh like crazy just thinking about it all. Grandma would have us go out on the porch to get her plants and take them into the house. That was the only time we were allowed on the patio. She loved them plants more than us, and it showed. She threatened us to make sure we did not break them.

Claudine or Robert did not have to worry about getting her plants because they were allowed outside to play, so they were nowhere to be found until the streetlights came on. It must have been nice to go where you wanted and play, free of stress. We did not get to experience that at all. When the streetlights came on, grandma would yell at us to take a bath and go to bed.

Grandma Mollie did attend church even though she was mean. She was such a hypocrite. I am glad grandma did not negatively shape my perspective about God. She and the neighbors were so holy on Sundays after all the hell she raised all week! She would worship, shout, and praise God in church, but the whole time couldn't wait to get home to gossip and play the lottery for the week.

She played gospel radio every morning at 6:00 am. Louise Williams was who she listened to from Monday to Sunday morning. While grandma would sing and praise God, she always yelled, "Don't make any noise when I'm giving God praise!" I always wondered what she was praising God for each day. Was it for a lottery win? Whenever grandma hit the number, she was filled with joy, saying, "Thank You, Lord. Thank You! You are so good to us, Lord." "Good to whom?" I would think to myself. We were getting the hell beat out of us, so she could not have been talking about Scholar and me. Grandma should have been praying for God to deliver her from all the craziness that was going on in her head. Maybe her heart could have received some of God's goodness. There was no good light of God shining in that house. Lots of times, some of the family didn't want to come over when we had gatherings. No one wanted to stick around once the liquor and beer came out on the table because they knew the drinkers would not behave themselves. There would always be a fight or argument.

The devil would raise his ugly head at each gathering. It was like he was sitting there with his fist under his chin, waiting and laughing because he knew he only needed one to fall prey to his tricks. It would always be Aunt Mary that stirred up the drama. She got drunk and brought up her sister's past, and there went the start of a fight. I could see the devil dripping spit and foaming at the mouth, saying, "Yes, my pitiful puppets. Fight and kill each other." Then the image would just fade away. My family was dysfunctional, and no one seemed to want to change. Therefore, Scholar and I were always trying to figure out who we were and even in the right family. "Lord, help us, please," I would say once I thought back over my life.

# CHAPTER 2
## *There Has To Be A Better Life*

Grandma Mollie scared us so bad that I would stutter when approached by her. Thank God I grew out of it because I hated stuttering. Just thinking about her coming for me was scary. When I couldn't get my words out fast enough, Grandma Mollie's big old basketball hands would go clean across my face! I would fall back a little, catch my balance, then pull myself back in the place to stand.

After Grandma Mollie got out of jail, she was a little different. She was quiet for the most part. I guess grandma needed something to shake her up to slow her down for a little. She was out of control, and I know that was God's way of getting her in order. Some days she would curse from sun-up to sun-down. She would even add discord in between her kids, turning them against one another. Yeah, grandma was the drama queen who loved drama. Drama made her day. She was always backbiting when people weren't around to hear how she felt about them, then smiling, laughing, and drinking with them like she never said one thing bad about them. Isn't that a blip? I just could not wrap my mind around this behavior. I guess I will never understand it because that was never my character.

Grandma Mollie had pull in the streets. Everyone respected her. She knew everybody, including the owners of the corner store, Mrs. and Mr. Green. They were the nosiest people I've ever seen. They saw and told everything! I remember Grandma Mollie sent me to the store one day to get a half-pound of beef bologna and a pound of cheese. Back then, things were cheap. As I placed the order with Mrs. Green, Mr. Green stood at the back of the store behind the thick glass in case of a robbery. No one would shoot them anyway because people seemed to have respect for them as well. The Greens had no problem going outside to receive deliveries such as bread, soda, etc.

While Mrs. Green was cutting the lunch meat, I decided to stick my hands in the freezer. That was where the pop sickles and ice cream sandwiches were. I decided to help myself this day. So, I took about two or three ice cream sandwiches, knowing I did not have the money to cover them. I figured no one would miss them. They had a whole lot of them, and I was sure they had some to spare. I slid them under my shirt, thinking no one saw me, but I did not know Mr. Green was watching the whole time. He never told his wife, Mrs. Green, but he called my grandma to let her know. I had no clue he even knew my grandma's number or even that he called. I paid for the food grandma sent me to the store and walked out happy that I got away with the ice cream sandwiches I stashed. At least, that's what I thought. Grandma Mollie was waiting for me on the porch, which was unusual. I just thought she was in a hurry to make the bologna sandwiches. I gave her the change from the twenty-dollar bill. Then she slapped me so hard that I thought I was going to fall. Grandma started checking my clothes and the ice cream sandwiches fell out from under my shirt.

She whipped the blood out of me with the extension cord. She grabbed me by my hair so I could not get away. Grandma called me a no-good sneaky little thief and told me how much she hated me for what I had done. I guess she felt I made her look bad because they knew she had money, so why couldn't I afford an ice cream sandwich? Grandma asked me why I stole the ice cream sandwiches, but I was too afraid to speak. As the pain ran across my body, I had nothing to say because I knew she would only continue to beat me no matter what I told her. Grandma asked me again why I stole the ice cream, and I told her I was hungry. She became offended and continued to yell at me. She claimed I should not have been hungry because she feeds me enough. I could beg to differ, but I did not want to get beat anymore, so I got quiet. Grandma Mollie beat me until she got tired then finally let me go. She told me to go to bed and not get up until she called me down to eat. That probably was the fastest I ever ran to my room. I could not stop crying because my body never experienced that much pain at once. My skin was covered in bleeding scars that stung as if I was covered in fire! She whipped me like a dog or as I was nothing. I felt slaves got better treatment than I did. I don't know if she was angry about something else before she got to me, but it seemed she went off in a rage. I just thank God I did not die. I thought she would never stop beating me. It took a long time for those scars to heal all over my body. I did not believe they would heal once I saw how detailed they were embedded in my skin. I accepted them at one point, but I am glad they are gone. I learned my lesson, and I never stole anything again, even if I was hungry.

Aunt Mary revisited us, and Grandma Mollie told her what I did to get into trouble. I guess I looked so bad that she didn't want to say anything to me. I don't know if Aunt Mary felt bad for me or did not feel like mocking me that day. She came over to get advice from grandma concerning her men friends. She always seemed to have difficulty with her guy friends, no matter how long or short they were together. It was the year 1978, and I remember Aunt Mary was dating Mr. Mike. He is dead now. When Mr. Mike was living, he was a fresh old man. He would always flirt with me, and I would keep my distance. I was just a kid, so what could he have possibly seen in me? I was twelve years old, quiet, and stayed to myself. I was not the fast promiscuous kid. Grandma would not have gone for that anyway. Therefore, I wondered why he would single me out. Aunt Mary would spend the night sometimes and allow Mr. Mike to stay over the house. I indeed kept my distance from him when he was around.

He stood about six-nine in height. He was a tall man. He always wore leathers, boots, headscarves, and his motorcycle vest or jacket. He rode a big old Harley Davis motorcycle. We knew whenever he was near because everyone could hear his bike a mile away. He would pull up, kick the kickstand down, then hop off his bike. We could hear him coming up the stairs with his black leather heavy boots hitting the steps one by one. Once he approached the top of the stairs, he would look down the hall at Scholar and me asking us to come to him. We had to say no because we were not allowed out of the room until grandma approved.

We were not in a hurry to go to him anyway, so we were not upset at all. He then went to the room. Aunt Mary stayed asking why we were always in the house, and the other kids were out playing. Aunt Mary told him to stay out of how grandma ran her home. She stated we were none of his concern then Mr. Mike got quiet, dropping the subject. They would shut the door to spend time together for a while. We stayed in our place as a child because we did not want to get beat for disrespecting grown folk's business. We stayed to ourselves and kept our mouths shut! Mr. Mike began visiting on the regular and started acting as he lived in grandma's house. One day, he came over, and I was going to the bathroom to do my business. When I came out, he was coming down the hall while Aunt Mary's door was closed.

He stopped and said, "You know you're pretty. You are going to make some man happy one day. You better watch out, girl!" I always wondered why he had an interest in me. I had no figure and was so skinny that my bowlegs stood out. I never thought I was pretty, especially after all grandma and Aunt Mary would say to me daily. I thought, why would any man want me when I got older? Mr. Mike laughed and went down the steps out the door after looking me up and down. He got on his loud motorcycle and left. I felt violated, but I never said anything to Aunt Mary about it. I knew she wouldn't believe me anyway. So, keeping quiet was the best thing to do.

The one person I did share everything with was Scholar so that she could watch herself around Mr. Mike. I trusted Scholar, so sharing secrets with her was safe. I didn't want anything to happen to her. She was and still is my baby sister. I had to look out for her, even if it meant taking a beating for her. Sometimes I did take a beating for her when the other kids would lie on her to get in trouble. They were so evil to us. Getting us in trouble was how they got their kicks and laughs for the day. When they singled Scholar out, I would say I did whatever it was. Most times, I did not know what I even agreed to take the blame for because I knew no one would hear my side anyway. I would take the whipping and go to my room to cry.

Mr. Mike continued to come around more and more. So, I would try my best to keep away from him because I felt uncomfortable around him. He was sneaky, and I could sense it. He always tried to find a way to get near me with his sly self. He would wait until no one was around and wander off to the bathroom, hoping to run into me. If all the grown folks were on the porch, he would find his way to the kitchen for a glass of water then sit in the living room waiting for me to come down. Once I saw him, I would turn around to hurry back upstairs without him seeing me. He would always see me and say, "Come sit on my lap. Come here. I just want to talk to you." I would freeze to see if he said something different, but it was always the same. As scared as I was, I knew better. I ran upstairs so fast and did not look back. I kept that a secret from my aunt as well. After a while, I guess he got the hint that I was not giving in to him, so he finally left me alone. Around the same time, Aunt Mary broke up with him. No one ever knew why.

She didn't keep a man too long anyway, so it was not out of the norm. I was filled with joy because that meant I never had to see Mr. Mike again. As time went on, Aunt Mary had many different men in and out of the house. Most of them were fresh old men that staired me up and down, but they never lasted long with Aunt Mary. I never understood why grown men wanted to sleep with little girls. They were all old, ugly, and nasty. They were old enough to be my father or granddaddy. It was all strange to me, very strange!

I had to carry these secrets for years because I knew in my heart that no one cared. They did not care about me, so I am sure they would not have cared about anything happening to me.

Thank God I did not have to deal with Grandma Mollie's men because she did not even allow them into her life. She would always say, "My money is my man. The only thing a man can do for me is pay my bills and give me a quick thrill." I guess she was not the settling down type after grandpa died, so she did not get close with men. Grandma was comfortable alone the rest of her life. No man ever came to visit her with flowers, and maybe she liked it that way.

Grandpa died when I was very young, they say. I never saw or met him. I sometimes thought grandpa's death was maybe the cause of her being so mean and wanting to be alone, so I tried to keep that in mind. Who knows? Perhaps she was born that way, and that was why grandpa died so soon. All I knew was Scholar, and I felt we were in prison minus the bars on the windows and shackles on our feet.

It felt like we were in a cave without light or running water and pain or noise that was never-ending. The noise was us screaming inside ourselves, hoping to be free. When folks came around and saw us, we smiled because we didn't want to give a clue to what was happening to us in that house. Therefore, if people spoke to us, we waited for grandma to allow us to speak. We didn't want to talk out of turn because the first thing grandma would say was, "don't be fresh!" We did not want to get in trouble, so we waited for her approval.

I remember asking grandma one day if Scholar and I could watch television in the living room. I don't know where the heart and confidence came from because I knew she did not allow us in that area. I asked anyway, and just like I thought, grandma said, "no," and sent me to my room. I guess she did not want us there in case her guest came over. I just figured she would say, "yes," because we were the only two keeping that area clean day and night. We cleaned, ran errands, etc., around the clock and never had the chance to enjoy life as a kid. It was crazy but our reality.

I remember one Saturday Uncle Alfonso came over to visit, and he started fussing at grandma because of the way he saw her treat us. He asked her why we couldn't go outside or watch television. Once Uncle Alfonso suggested she allow us to do one or the other, grandma told him, no, and they began to fuss at each other. Uncle Alfonso got so frustrated that he shook his head in disappointment and left. We stayed in our room that day because we did not want grandma to take her anger out on us. That day went by quickly. Even after we ate dinner, we went back to our room and got ready for bed. We knew Uncle Alfonso was just trying to help, but we did not want any problems from grandma. Our other siblings were still outside with the grown folks' grandma said she did not want us around.

Shockingly the next day, Uncle Alfonso returned to talk to Grandma Mollie about him and his wife Danielle raising Scholar and me. Grandma told him that he could take me, but not Scholar because she would not let the SSI check go. I did not want to leave Scholar and felt terrible that grandma would not allow her to come along with me. All I could think about was my freedom. I needed to get out of that house by any means necessary.

I felt like that was the happiest day of my life. It was like the sky opening, and God reminded me that he never forgot about me and had a plan the whole time. I was so bubbly inside and just wanting to scream for joy! I could probably do a headstand or something I had never done at that moment. I didn't want to leave my little sister knowing all the stuff that went on in that house. I thought, "What could I do to make things better if I stayed?" Nothing! We would have remained in prison together. If Grandma Mollie decided to beat us, it would happen, and no one could stop it.

I imagined us as weak creatures that Grandma Mollie took control of with her magical powers, and no one could get away even if they tried. I figured this was my moment to break free. Scholar cried and begged me not to leave her, but I saw a way of escape and needed to take it. I decided to go, and Scholar was crushed. Maybe things would change, and grandma would allow her to join me eventually. Grandma told me to go with Uncle Alfonso but not to take anything with me that she brought. None of it was worth anything, nor was it much that she got. The clothes grandma gave Scholar and me were not nice at all, and she did not care.

Uncle Alfonso took me home with him. Aunt Danielle was waiting for me to arrive. I tried to be strong and not break down, although I wanted to. Scholar was all I had. All we had was each other. I missed her and had only been gone for a moment. As we drove away that day, I wondered how long she sat and cried for me to come back. I knew Uncle Alfonso was only trying to help and do right by us, but a piece of me died that day. I knew I felt death while staying at grandma's house, but I had Scholar by my side to keep me going. I was by her side to keep her going. Who would be by her side now? Who would play pretend with her? Who would help her clean the house? Who would she talk to while shut up in the room now? I prayed for freedom, but why did it hurt so bad? I did not want to regret being set free from prison. I just knew I had to get out of that house. It was all I prayed for to happen.

Once I arrived at my uncle's house, it felt strange being there without Scholar. They even had rules for me to follow, but it was ok because I felt safe. I wanted a new life. I desired to be liked and loved all at the same time. I knew Scholar loved me even if no one else did. I just wanted more, I guess. When it was time for dinner, Aunt Danielle already knew I was hungry. I was grateful to have enough food to eat. Aunt Danielle ran my bathwater and laid out a long T-shirt for me to wear for bed. She knew grandma did not allow me to bring much. I almost came with nothing, just the clothes on my back. I did not care, as long as I got away. After my bath, she showed me to my bedroom. They had a two-bedroom apartment, with the second one not in use. Before Aunt Danielle left the bedroom, she asked me about the scars all over my back and arms. I told her grandma beat Scholar and me whenever and with whatever she wants. I even told her grandma calls us ugly. Aunt Danielle dropped her head in disappointment.

She looked so sad for us. I could see the tears forming in her eyes, but she held them back like a soldier fighting in battle, watching others die. She asked me if I knew how to pray, and I told her I did. She wanted us to pray together and for me to start it off. I began to pray, "Dear God, I know You brought me here to this new place. I want to say thank you. God, please, please keep Scholar. Protect her from my grandma. Don't let grandma hurt her. I thank you for my new life, Amen." Aunt Danielle hugged me, and I got in bed. She pulled the covers over me and said goodnight. Off to sleep, I went.

That was on a Sunday when I left Grandma Mollie's house. Monday morning, there was a knock on my bedroom door. I said, come in, not knowing if it was Uncle Alfonso or Aunt Daniel. Uncle Alfonso entered and asked if I was ok and if I slept ok. He told me to wash my face and brush my teeth to prepare for breakfast. They had everything I needed, as if they knew I would live with them one day. I could smell the fresh bacon in the air. I didn't know if it was pork or not, but I knew it was not the smell of fatback that grandma would make every morning. I was ok with that and ready to eat.

I came downstairs and sat in the living room. I did not want to be disrespectful or intrude, so I sat there until Uncle Alfonso or Aunt Danielle called me into the kitchen. Aunt Danielle asked me why I was in the living room and to come to the kitchen. I told her I wanted to be respectable and wait to be called. My plate was waiting on the table for me. It was cheese eggs, bacon, grits, and toast with butter and jelly on it. My mouth watered because it all looked so good. Aunt Danielle said grace over our food, and we ate. No one spoke at that moment because we were busy eating. Everyone finished eating, and my uncle and aunt had to go off to work. They told me not to open the door or answer the phone for anyone. Back then, everyone had a house phone. Today that is a thing of the past. I did what they asked of me. They both had to work a lot, but it was okay because I knew right from wrong. I was not afraid to be alone either. Grandma used to leave Scholar and me alone in the house regularly. Therefore, it did not matter to me. I was happy to sit and watch television without anyone telling me to go to my room. I felt like a queen.

There were times I thought about Scholar. I wondered if she was doing ok. I wanted to know what was happening to her there. Was she eating enough food? Was our oldest brother and sister picking on her? They treated her so horrible. I hated when they picked on her, calling her names like black. They would always say she was black as ink, and all they could see was her teeth. No one came to her rescue but me back then. I was sure no one helped her after I moved.

I continually prayed and never forgot about Scholar. I would always ask God to touch grandma's heart so she could send Scholar with me to Uncle Alfonso's house. I wanted her to experience real love, and, in the meantime, I asked God to keep Scholar protected. Aunt Danielle would get home from work first. They had a son they raised together from Uncle Alfonso's past relationship. His mother would watch him while my uncle and aunt were at work then drop her off once they got home. He was just a baby, not yet walking.

Aunt Danielle would ask how my day was, and I would always say I was praying for Scholar. She told me they wanted Scholar to join us, but grandma would have to allow it. Aunt Danielle told me to keep praying for my sister and grandma also. She would say to me never have hate in my heart towards anyone because I would be mean and hateful just as they were. She wanted me to forgive my grandma for what she had done to my sister and me because God sees all. He sees what goes on in the dark. God will bring it out to the light. None of us gets away with anything in this world. "It will get better for you both one day," Aunt Danielle would say. I prayed in my mind and asked God to search my heart to see if I forgave grandma or not. I felt as if I did, but just in case, I forgave her again anyway. I even forgave Aunt Marry because she played a part as well. I even forgave the fresh nasty old men Aunt Marry was dating. I forgave my sister Claudine and brother Robert too! I knew I was free from them all, so why not forgive. I didn't know if I could forgive so quickly because I was living in a new place or because it was time. Maybe a little of both, but I felt another level of freedom hit me.

I lived with Uncle Alfonso for a couple of years. I loved the clothes they would buy me. They brought me the prettiest dresses and pants. They even set my socks to match what I wore. Aunt Danielle treated me like the daughter she never had. She taught me how to cook and bake, but I was never good at baking. I could cook a little because of what I learned from Grandma Mollie. Grandma made me sit in the kitchen with her every time she would cook. Now, I don't just cook, but I'm a cook to this day. I must say that hard times in my life paid off.

Aunt Danielle even gave me a party when my birthday came around. It was all new for me because grandma had never done that. It wasn't many people there. It was Aunt Danielle's nieces, mother, Uncle Alfonso, and the baby. His name is Alfonso Jr., and he is so handsome. I remember him not crying a lot. Aunt Danielle would allow me to hold him sometimes. I was grateful to have my first birthday party. My party was a hit, even though there were just a few in attendance. I wished Scholar could've been there for my party too. That would have made my birthday even more special.

I missed Scholar like crazy, but I tried to enjoy my stay in the new place. Grandma Mollie heard how nice they treated me, and the devil began to use her and Aunt Mary. Grandma Mollie decided to take me back to her house. She did this about three different times. She went back and forward with me as if she did not know if she wanted me to stay with Uncle Alfonso or not.

Aunt Danielle and Uncle Alfonso would treat me like a queen, and that devil would use Grandma Mollie and Aunt Marry to take me away from Uncle Alfonso. It never failed. The only good thing out of it all was that I got to see Scholar again, but nothing had changed in that house. Grandma was still that nasty mean old lady. She continued to pick on Scholar. I knew in my heart that I was next in line to be her victim. I would sit and wonder if Aunt Danielle and Uncle Alfonso were thinking of me. Uncle Alfonso stopped visiting grandma's house because he disagreed with what she was doing. I guess Uncle Alfonso got tired of fighting with her. He knew she was evil.

There go my birthday celebrations out the window. I'll never see another cake or ice cream again. It was fun while it lasted, I thought. I had to be thankful that I got even to experience a party. I was thirteen years of age, and Scholar was twelve years old. Grandma Mollie was getting up in age also and could no longer care for us. One day she was in the kitchen cooking breakfast and said to Scholar and me, "You both are going to live with your Aunt Glenda." We were so happy to hear that! Anything was better than living with grandma. We replied, "ok," but was bursting with joy on the inside. Grandma responded, "Don't get happy because I make you stay here with me! Also, don't go telling her what goes on in my house with your nappy-headed selves. If you know what's best for you both, you will keep your mouths shut!"

We dropped our heads and kept eating our breakfast. I was so giggly inside, singing to myself in a quiet voice. I thought, "Oh yea, we are leaving this house! Oh yea, we are leaving this crazy house! No more Grandma Mollie." Grandma asked me what I was singing, but I told her nothing. I did not want her to get upset. We hurried up eating so we could start getting our things together. That was the one day she didn't have to rush us to eat. We ate as fast as we could. We could not wait to leave that house. Thank God Scholar could join me this time. I was so happy that God answered my prayers again.

Aunt Glenda came the next day to pick us up. She talked about Jesus all the time. She always said everyone in her house would serve the Lord. So, we knew to be on our best behavior in her home. Aunt Glenda was so pretty and tall. She had long, gorgeous thick hair, thick eyebrows, and wide round eyes. Aunt Glenda had the most stunning teeth. We could tell she took care of herself. She did not wear pants either or allowed us to wear them. Aunt Glenda went to church three times a week. Tuesday night bible study, Friday night worship, and Sunday service. She asked if we knew Jesus, and we told her we did not. We knew of Jesus but did not know Him. All we knew was that we saw grandma praise God one minute, then the next, the devil was using her. That was our glimpse of what Jesus could have possibly meant. Years later, we found out grandma's behavior was not even a touch of Jesus, and we were happy it was not.

Scholar and I were out of that wicked woman's house. We didn't mind going to church at all with Aunt Glenda if it meant leaving grandma's house. We didn't see daylight at grandma's house unless she had us go to the store for her or bring her plants in from the porch. Therefore, going to church was a treat for us. We did not mind one bit. Aunt Glenda brought us dresses to wear, and we threw away our pants. She meant what she said about us not wearing pants in her house. Aunt Glenda was a servant of the Lord because she gave herself and did what she could for others. She took us in, and we were grateful.

She had healthy rules in her house that we were happy to follow. Breakfast and dinner were served at a specific time, and Scholar and I had to be seated together at the table. We said grace before we ate and had enough time to eat. There was no name-calling allowed in the house, and that made us feel safe around her even more. She really cared for us. I loved how she would make she we were always clean and did our hair with big ribbons. Sometimes the dresses were pretty, and others looked a little crazy with all the colors and patterns on them. So many flowers with big bows all over the dress! I don't know if she thought we were back in the '70s or what, but around this time, it was the early 80's, so that was out of style. We did not say anything about the dresses because we were just happy to have something new.

We had been at Aunt Glenda's house for a little while, and things seemed to be going well until it wasn't. Aunt Glenda had a flip side to her that we would have never guessed. It was like grandma number two, and she was just as crazy as her mother. When Aunt Glenda said we would serve the Lord in her house, we did not know what she meant by that. We just went along with it, so we did not have to go back to grandma's house. She made us get up before breakfast to washing our faces and brushing our teeth. Then she would tell us to get on our knees and terry (call out the name "Jesus" repeatedly) to receive the Holy Ghost. We knew nothing about Jesus or the Holy Ghost. Therefore, we had no idea why we had to do it or what we were even doing. She made us do this consistently. We would terry but never got the Holy Ghost, as she would say. We would be down on our knees for hours. We were tired and hungry, wondering how serving the Lord tied into it all.

One day we were on our knees so long that I asked Aunt Glenda if we could take a break to eat because I was so hungry. She looked at me crazy and said I was being "fresh" or sarcastic. I honestly wasn't at all. I was being honest, but I felt I should not have said anything after the fact. Before I knew it, Aunt Glenda went to her room and returned with a long brown extension cord. She began to beat me and turned to Scholar to beat her too. She told Scholar she was getting a beating for being sneaky, and she wanted to beat the Holy Ghost into both of us. Aunt Glenda told us to repeat the name "Jesus" repeatedly while she beat us, but we could not get it out outside of the screaming we did because it hurt so bad. I thought to myself, "Why we had to keep ending up with crazy evil family members?" Was this serving the Lord? If so, I don't want it anymore. She beat us both until her arms got tired. Then she told us to wash our faces and sit at the table. We ate, then she sent us to our room to lay down. I knew we were in the pits of Hell all over again.

What kind of stuff did Grandma Mollie tell Aunt Glenda about us? Aunt Glenda was under the impression that we were demons, and she was determined to beat them out of us. She would always say she would beat the Holy Ghost into us because grandma already warned her about us. At that moment we were so afraid. Everything shifted from a safe place to a house of terror. Scholar and I started to pray like never before. We would ask God to send somebody to help us. We were prisoners again and needed to be rescued. We may not have known all about Jesus, but we knew prayer worked. We did not stop praying, no matter what happened to us. We were in fear of getting hurt bad, and no one would ever know. We needed a savior and hoped that God would send them quickly.

# CHAPTER 3
## There Today, Gone Tomorrow

Aunt Glenda also had a son, and his name is Randell. He was five years of age at the time. She loved him a lot, and she always made it known through her actions. She spoiled him so much, and Randell could do whatever he wanted. She treated him as if he was still a baby. He was quiet but very sneaky. He would do things then lie about doing it, like going into the refrigerator without permission. He would eat snacks, and Scholar and I would get the blame. He would not confess to it, so Aunt Glenda would side with him and beat us.

I look back sometimes and think my family just had a thing for beating on us. It sounds crazy, but it seemed that way. Aunt Glenda would go to church some evenings for bible study and Friday nights worship but leave all of us home. It was strange because she always had us in church with her. We did not mind staying home. Randell would be friendly to us when she was gone. I guess he knew his mother was not there to protect him, but we weren't trying to hurt him or mistreat him. We are family, and family should stick together, we thought. There was so much hate in my family between my aunts and uncles that they never did anything together. Grandma Mollie did not seem to care.

When Aunt Glenda would leave us home, I would make our dinner. It was nothing fancy, just peanut butter and jelly sandwiches most of the time. It was quick and easy for me as a child. Yes, only thirteen, so I stayed in a child's place as I was told. Aunt Glenda would get in from church around 10:00 pm. There would be nothing to report, so we went to bed to get ready for whatever was in store for us the next day.

The months were moving fast. It was the summertime, and we didn't do anything but church. She didn't trust us to go outside. We lived in the projects of the ghetto on the ninth floor. It was scary living in that neighborhood, so we understood why we could not go outside. The lights would blow out frequently. The elevator would never work, and we had to carry the groceries up nine flights of steps, not to mention the laundry! She did not have a washer and dryer in her apartment. I began to believe Aunt Glenda just wanted us with her to become her little maids. Once we moved in with her, she handed all the housework over to Scholar and me.

Aunt Glenda would even have me cooking. I fried chicken and made canned vegetables. She brought the good part of the chicken, the breast. Scholar and I never had chicken breast until we moved in with her, and we were grateful for that experience. She didn't have a problem making sure food was in the house, so we always ate well.

I remember this one particular time we all woke up around 9 AM. I wondered why Aunt Glenda did not have Scholar and me up cooking and cleaning before that time. That was strange because Aunt Glenda always had us up extra early. I thought maybe she was tired, sick, or just being nice to us that day. When Scholar, Randell, and I went into the hallway, we saw a tall, handsome, brown-skinned man exit her bedroom. Aunt Glenda followed behind him and introduced him to us. My eyes got big with surprise, and my mouth fell to the floor. Scholar just had this crazy confused look on her face as if she did not know what was going on. Randell was only five, so he didn't care. Aunt Glenda was smiling ear to ear, heading to the kitchen to make breakfast. I guess she wanted to show him that she could cook.

The tall man's name is Roy. He was a member of Bethlehem Temple Church that Aunt Glenda attended. I knew we had seen that man before, but I was not too sure of the location. He was one of the deacons that sat on the front row of the church. I just shook my head with confusion, thinking what Elder and Mother Tucker would say when they found this out. Aunt Glenda had told us that God shows Elder Tucker things that are right and wrong in the house of God. So, I knew God would reveal Aunt Glenda and Roy to him. To our surprise, that was not even the whole story! After breakfast, Aunt Glenda told us they were getting married and having a baby together. Therefore, this relationship had been going on for some time.

They got married, and Aunt Glenda told us to address him as Brother Roy. Brother Roy was nice. He looked out for Scholar and me. He started seeing the real side of his wife when she would make us terry and slap us in our faces because we didn't terry fast enough. Brother Roy would ask her why she hit us like that. Brother Roy would also ask her why she did not make her son terry and hit him too. Aunt Glenda would always respond to him, saying he did not have any say when it came to Scholar and me. Before we went to our room, I told Uncle Roy that Randell had the Holy Ghost already, so he did not have to terry. I walked away and slammed our room door in frustration.

We realized Brother Roy was our uncle since he married our aunt, so Scholar and I started calling him Uncle Roy. He cared more for us than she did. So, when Randell would do something and lie on us, Uncle Roy would get a thin leather belt and whip Randell. He didn't believe in extension cords. Thank God Uncle Roy started realizing we were not treated fairly, and I was so happy he was there to help us. We thought maybe God sent him according to our prayers. We thanked God every day.

One Monday morning, we were all up early, just as any other day, but Aunt Glenda was talking on the phone. I knew it was only Sister Pat because they were very close. Aunt Glenda told her how she would get Scholar's social security check and save all she received to buy herself a new house. Aunt Glenda had no idea I could hear her conversation. I was disappointed but did not put anything past any of my family members regarding money.

Back then, they did not charge a lot to put down on the house, so it would not have taken her long to go through the housing process. Well, I had a trick for her because I was not going to allow that to happen. I waited for her to leave for the day, and I called Grandma Mollie. I don't know where I got the confidence from, but I needed grandma to know what Aunt Glenda was planning behind her back. I told grandma everything Aunt Glenda did to Scholar and me and what she planned for Scholar's checks. Many might why I called Grandma Mollie when she was an abuser as well. I knew Aunt Glenda's plan was wrong, and honestly, living with grandma was better than staying with Aunt Glenda. Living with grandma was prison and death also but living with Aunt Glenda, we feared for our lives. We knew grandma did not have a problem with sending Aunt Mary to pick us up. Aunt Glenda did not mess with Aunt Mary at all. We wanted to leave Aunt Glenda's house and could not wait to go.

Aunt Glenda found out what I said to grandma, and she became very angry with me. She started fussing at me and called me the devil. Uncle Roy was still at work and had not returned home yet. Therefore, he could not help me with this situation. She was furious because her plans for a new house just went out the window. She told me it was all my fault and that we were going back to grandma's house. We did not care, though. We were ready to get out of her house. Aunt Glenda would not stop yelling, and I started sweating heavily because I was nervous about what she might do. It felt as if I had heavy rocks in my shoes that prevented me from moving. Before I knew it, Aunt Glenda charged at me like a bull in a bullfight. I envisioned horns growing out of her head and steam shooting out of her nostrils! She got in my face asking me why I told on her, and fear took over, and I began to stutter. I could not form a word at all. See, I had gotten up just enough courage to tell my Grandma Mollie what was said, but I couldn't get up the nerve to say to Aunt Glenda why I did it.

She knocked me down on the couch and called me dumb. She reminded me of how her mother did not care about Scholar and me and that she beat the blood out of us regularly. She was right, but we did not care because Aunt Glenda did the same thing to us. Aunt Glenda told us to get out of her sight and pack our clothes. She told us Aunt Mary would pick us up that following day and not to expect any breakfast. Aunt Glenda told us to let our grandma feed us. I would never have thought she would've gone that low, but she did. We should have expected anything at that point. We had been treated worse, so it did not move our emotions.

Uncle Roy returned home, and Aunt Glenda shared with him what I said to Grandma Mollie. I guess she wanted him to be upset with me as well. He seemed not to even care about the whole thing, so Aunt Glenda just dropped it. She called us into the kitchen to eat dinner. Thank God we were able to get dinner at least. Aunt Glenda was still fussing about it at the dinner table. Uncle Roy asked her to let it go so that we could enjoy dinner, but the eye-rolling kept coming. When we were done eating, Scholar and I cleaned the kitchen. We thought to ourselves this was the last time we would clean her kitchen. I was cleaning and singing to myself with joy. "Yes, Jesus Loves Me" was the song that came to mind. I didn't know a lot about Jesus, but I felt the need to sing that part repeatedly. We took our baths and went to bed. Aunt Mary was picking us up early, and we were ready to go.

Aunt Mary knocked on the door the following day, and Aunt Glenda let her in. Aunt Mary greeted her and asked if we were ready. Aunt Glenda didn't speak back, but no one seemed to care. We grabbed our bags, and out the door we went. Aunt Mary questioned me in the car about what happened between Aunt Glenda and grandma. So, I told her, and she laughed to herself, saying how Aunt Glenda will not get Scholar's check for her a house. Aunt Mary drove a big green thunderbird car. It was shiny and pretty. She drove like a mad man, which was fast! Aunt Mary told us to sit back and not to move. We were praying the whole time in the back seat, rocking from side to side. She loved her car so much that she dressed it up with different things. One thing Aunt Mary added to her car was hydraulics. She told us to watch the trick it could do, and she would make the car jump up and down. It was creepy and fun at the same time. It felt like being on a roller coaster. That's what I imagined in my head.

We pulled up to grandma's front door. We didn't want to be there, but what other choice did we have? Grandma was sitting on the porch drinking a cup of coffee. We walked up the steps, and she never said hello. Grandma just looked at us and said, put our bags in the room and eat. Aunt Glenda told grandma she was not feeding us breakfast. So, we put our clothes away and sat down in the kitchen to eat. We knew to be on our best behavior, so we did not make grandma upset. Although we hardly ever stepped out of line. We were more afraid of grandma than Aunt Glenda. After washing our plates, and headed to our room. I knew Grandma Mollie was still going to remain her evil self even after I told her the plans of Aunt Glenda. We knew it would kill her to be nice to us. That was out of the picture, nor did we get our hopes up.

Scholar and I went back to the way things were, which was playing make-believe. We brought our beautiful castle back to the forefront of our minds. This time we had yummy white icing cakes, lemon cookies, and hot cocoa to snack on while enjoying the sun and birds sing. There were even rose bushes planted in the garden of our castle. Scholar and I danced around in our room as if we did not have a care in the world. Dancing was our favorite thing to do in our castle. Our castle was big and trimmed with gold and a touch of silver. The pretend life was what Scholar and I dreamed of when we felt we were locked away in a cage or prison at grandma's house.

We hated it there but thanked God it was not Aunt Glenda's house anymore. Grandma ended up losing her house due to non-payment of taxes. Grandma left Aunt Mary in charge of paying the taxes, and she never followed through. I guess when they say, "God don't like ugly," this was indeed an example. We had to start over in a new part of town. Claudine and Robert knew a few people there, so they were okay with the transition. Scholar and I had never seen anyone or played outside to make friends, so it did not bother us.

We were on a block that had few houses and a dry cleaners on the corner. It was quiet all the time and boring. The same rules applied for Scholar and me, cleaning and staying in the house. There was no laundromat near us, so we had to wash the dirty clothes in the bathtub. Three washes and a rinse in the tub, then we hung them out on the line in the back yard. Grandma Mollie made Claudine and Robert help us out. There were a lot of clothes that needed to be washed. We were washing for everyone in the house. Thank God He touched grandma's mind and heart to see that it would have been too much for Scholar and me to do it alone.

It was the summertime and extremely hot outside. Grandma would send us to the store to get little stuff like milk, bread, and butter. She would also have us get starch in the blue and white box, which she loved to eat. I sometimes wondered if that played a part in her having diabetes. Grandma Mollie had gotten to know the store owner, Mr. Berry, in our new neighborhood. He was nice. Whenever grandma needed something but didn't have the money right away, Mr. Berry would allow us to take it on credit. He would keep track of the items in his black book. Mr. Berry would then give me a receipt for grandma and send me back home. When grandma's check came in the mail, she and Claudine would go to the check cashing location to get it cashed. She would pay Mr. Berry so she could run another "tab" when needed. Check cashing day was usually the happiest day of grandma's life. It arrived on the first day of every month.

I recall grandma and Claudine calling the social security department to lie about not receiving the check just to get another one. Back then, social security agents seemed not to care as much as they do now. Grandma Mollie would always get a second check when she called to report a missing check. Grandma would use it to pay off other "tabs" she had, play street lottery numbers, and buy food. She would never bless God or His church house with any money even though He allowed her to get the extra cash.

Grandma would bless Reverend Ike with some money when she could. He was a well-known preacher. She would expect a massive blessing in return, but it never happened because they were both snakes! Grandma was stealing that money, and Reverend Ike was a liar. That man was lying so much that he was flying. He may as well dressed in two lefts shoes, a pair of dark sunglasses, and backward clothes while he spoke. Reverend Ike was always shining with fancy diamonds and rubies brought with the money folks had mailed him. It was sad, but that was who my family trusted and believed. Folks put more faith in that man than God. Reverend Ike would wear pink suits, and he drove a pink Cadillac taking poor desperate people's money.

Many followed this man. He was a false prophet getting rich off what the people wanted to hear. He was not speaking the truth, and the people couldn't see that, especially Grandma Mollie. She would write letters to him to receive numbers to play the lottery. Although God is not in gambling, I'm not going to lie, grandma would win big money from those numbers. Just know the devil can grant our desires too, but it is cursed. The curse is for us to reap lack so we can keep coming back for more. The devil has to stay in business somehow. We often sell out to the devil instead of trusting God, but that is another story for another day. When grandma wins would slow down from the numbers the Reverend sent her, she would go to her dream book with many colors. This book had some of everything in it, and she trusted it to use the numbers within. We would know when grandma had enough with the lottery because she would be grumpy and upset, yelling about the amount of money she lost. She would always say she was done with gambling but someway find an urge to run back to play. I was convinced grandma was addicted to gambling. The trick of the enemy took over, and she kept going back for more. That was the typical routine we saw.

Speaking of typical, life was a cycle that did not change. Grandma collected the mail this one day, and she walked back into the house angry. Scholar and I figured we should stay clear of her so she did not take it out on us as she usually would. She announced that we received an eviction notice due to non-payment of the rent. Everyone looked confused except Aunt Mary. She had done it again! Aunt Mary neglected to pay the rent and did not even tell grandma she fell behind. The landlord told us we had one month to move out. Grandma Mollie had to save her check and ask for help from the family. Once Aunt Emma and Aunt Laney found out, they put money together to help grandma move. Grandma Mollie would keep putting her trust in Aunt Mary. Why? No one will ever know!

We only lived in that house for about seven months. Grandma never had a problem finding a new place. I was just tired of packing and unpacking. Grandma found a home with the help of Aunt Mary. It was on a tiny block with lots of kids. We never lived on a small block before, so it was going to be interesting. All we were wondering was would the other kids on the block accept us. Scholar and I did not have too much to worry about because grandma did not allow us out to play.

Aunt Mary found a school for all of us. We started school a month or so after we moved. West Philadelphia High School was the place I had to attend. I wasn't sure if I wanted to graduate from that school or not, but I knew I would be there for some time. Grandma brought Claudine and Robert new clothes for the school year, while Aunt Emma looked out for Scholar and me. We were so grateful for her kindness because we knew grandma was not going to buy us anything. We would have had to continue wearing the clothes we had, which were ripped and too small. Talk about being the black sheep of the family! That was indeed Scholar and me. I never understood why Grandma Mollie did not buy Scholar new clothes. She deserved new stuff because grandma was getting a big check for her every month. Scholar did not see much of the money, and there was nothing anyone could do about it. Grandma dared anyone to try. Aunt Emma would visit us to do me and Scholar's hair so we could look decent leaving out for school. I thank God for her because she felt sorry for us, even Aunt Laney. Aunt Laney would stay to herself because she did not want her kids around the hatful conditions of being at grandma's house, and I did not blame her. We did not want to be there either, but we had no choice!

Scholar was in junior high and couldn't seem to cope with being there. She was terrified to go to school. Grandma had her placed in special classes, and I believe that was what bothered her the most. The school principal ended up scheduling a meeting with Grandma Mollie and Aunt Mary about putting Scholar in a special school altogether. Grandma and Aunt Mary agreed, so

Scholar had to take the yellow bus to another school every morning. It's crazy because the school was around the corner from grandma's old house and lost because Aunt Mary did not pay the taxes. The school had a wall around it as if it was a prison. I thought of it as a big scary dungeon that held evil people with no return home. I overheard grandma say the school had people of all ages, young and old, with all kinds of problems.

Grandma said Scholar would fit right in because she was crazy too, but Scholar wasn't crazy. Scholar was going through mentally because of all the trauma she faced in life. All the things grandma and others had done to her began to take a toll on her. Grandma knew what was happening, but she did not want to take responsibility for any of it. Grandma fooled many people into thinking she cared about us, but she did not at all. She treated us horribly. Grandma and Aunt Mary abused us physically, mentally, emotionally. We even had spiritual about from Aunt Glenda. We always thought to ourselves why we deserved that type of treatment. Our other siblings even treated us like trash. I felt we might not have even been real family the way they all treated Scholar and me. I knew our mom and dad were off in the world on their journey and process, but what if they had their stuff together and could take us back? Would life be different for Scholar and me? Would we still be the black sheep of the family? I guess it was never for us to find out.

Grandma's diabetes would fluctuate a lot, and sometimes she would need insulin or a pill to keep her balanced. Somedays, grandma, could not do it independently and needed Scholar and me to help her. If we did not help her, she could have gone into a diabetic coma and possibly died. As many times we had opportunities to do her wrong, we couldn't go through with the thought. We did love her despite all she had done to us. That's where we were different, and we tried our hardest not to be like her. Grandma was up in age and could not get around to paying the bills, so she trusted Aunt Mary again. Aunt Mary failed again with keeping up with the rent and had to move again. We realized Aunt Mary was addicted to alcohol, and that was where most of the money was going. Aunt Mary would drink from sun-up to sundown. Alcohol was an expensive habit to upkeep. She would drink so much that she stopped getting drunk! Aunt Mary would have black-out moments that would cause her to sleep for long periods.

I do not think Aunt Mary cared that we had to keep moving because of her, but grandma sure did not say anything to her either. We packed and moved again. This time on the other side of town, but grandma kept us at the same schools. Grandma Mollie used a family member's address, so we did not have to change schools. I had turned fourteen, and Scholar was now thirteen years old. Grandma had us to start taking the bus to school. She brought bus tokens for us, and since Aunt Mary worked for the bus company, she gave us bus tokens. Yes, Aunt Mary was addicted to alcohol and drove the public transportation that carried hundreds of people each day, including us. That did not stop her from drinking. I guess they hired anyone back then.

Grandma Mollie's health started to deteriorate slowly. Honestly, Scholar and I were kind of happy. We didn't want to sound heartless, but her health hindered her from beating us as much. When she would attempt to beat us, she would get really weak and have to stop. Although she could not beat us as much, the mental and emotional abuse did not stop. I knew God was up to something, but what? We took whatever small victories we could. There were times grandma would call Aunt Mary over to beat us because she was strong. She was strong as a man. We hated to see her coming! We were just appreciative that the physical abuse was not every day anymore. There were times I would cry out to God, asking Him to show Grandma Mollie that we loved her before she died. I was not sure if she would have believed it, though, but it was worth a try. We even did extra chores around the house to get grandma to see our love for her, but that did not work. She was set in her ways, so we just accepted that.

When I was finally able to work, I got my working papers from school, and grandma signed them. I was determined to make my own money since it was never given to me. Scholar could not work because grandma said she was slow, so her monthly checks would not stop. I worked at a candy store but did not make much. Another job offer opened at the school, and I took it cleaning the school and the baseball field. I worked with six others and was able to make friends, which felt great. I wished Scholar could have had the same experience, but I knew it was only a matter of time. I just needed her to be patient.

After school let out for the summer, I became a full-time working woman. I had tremendous responsibility and was getting paid for my time. I had to give grandma half my check because that was her rule for people with a job living in her house. I did not have a problem with it. I just hated working hard only to have a hundred dollars to spend out of a three-hundred-dollar check! Grandma took over half of my check, and I was the one out in the hot sun most of the day cleaning the field and then cleaning inside the school building for hours! I would get home and still have to clean, so I was always tired.

Grandma Mollie decided to buy a house, so we had to move again. This time grandma was sure to keep track of all the bills, so we did not get evicted by surprise again. Things were still the same even in that house. Grandma did not care that we were up in age or that I had a job. We still had to slave doing chores and could not go outside. We knew chores were our portion, but we wanted to go outside like the other kids. Grandma's health began decreasing again. We knew she was not her usual self when she would stop sitting out on the porch as much. So, whenever grandma didn't feel her best, Scholar and I would sneak outside to sit on the porch for a little. Trouble came when Claudine and Robert caught us on the porch and knew we did not get grandma's permission. They told grandma on us, and she cursed us out severely. She even called Aunt Mary over to slap us around. Grandma Mollie was too weak to beat us; therefore, she turned us over to Aunt Mary. In the meantime, we had to sit in grandma's room until Aunt Mary showed up. That was the norm, so it did not phase us anymore.

# CHAPTER 4
## Who Am I?

The new house grandma brought was breathtaking. I almost forgot we lived in Philadelphia, PA, because of how nice it was. Philadelphia is not the best place to live, but it is manageable in some parts of the city. I remember Aunt Mary telling grandma she would pay off the house and keep it when she passed away. We knew Aunt Mary would not pay off anything to save her life. Grandma told her she would live a long time and she was not going anywhere. Grandma Mollie was not trying to hear what Aunt Mary was talking about as far as her house.

We all have a death date that was written at the beginning of time. We might not know the day or hour, but it is all a part of life. None of us can stop it; therefore, we should make the best of it while we are living. We watched grandma get sicker over the years. The sad part was only one of her daughters checked on her to see if she needed help. Aunt Mary moved her son into grandma's house, and Claudine and Robert began to get into trouble in the streets. Aunt Mary's son was no different.

Grandma's house spun out of control, but they made sure they beat Scholar and me to keep us in alignment. Our sister, Claudine, started getting into trouble with the law, and Grandma Mollie would bail her out every time with no problem. I don't even think she asked her any questions. If that were Scholar and me, we would have gotten our heads knocked off! That's how it was in that house. Scholar and I were the nobodies of the family.

I found myself falling into depression and needed an outlet. Life was moving so fast, but I felt as if I was standing still. I thought I had no purpose and just existing until it was time for me to die. One of our family members started stopping over from time to time. They were there to spend some time with grandma then leave. One day grandma stepped out, and they asked if I wanted to try some cocaine. At first, I was hesitant, but they told me it would help me cope with life. That was enough for me, and I was willing to try the cocaine. Dealing with life was all I desired, and that was my moment. I would have never guessed that the family member that introduced me to cocaine was using it for themselves. I later found out that they introduced my other sister and brother, Claudine, and Robert to cocaine before me. The family member told me all about them both getting high all the time.

I grew comfortable with the family member and started buying the drugs from them. Whenever grandma would start her abuse, I would get high off the drugs and not even worry about what she was saying. Cocaine became my best friend. I could count on it every time to block out anything I was dealing with that day. Scholar did not want to try it, and I was glad about it. I knew it was not good to do, but in those moments, I felt as if it helped me to live another day. I thought about taking my own life sometimes, but I had the cocaine to help pull me through those dark moments. Cocaine killed me slowly, but it gave me comfort as I got high. I was addicted to comfort because I never had that in my life. I held on to the cocaine and needed more and more. I had an addiction that I had to pay for, so I had to keep a job. I went from one job to another. I worked, cashed my check, and brought drugs. I mean, God was blessing me with multiple jobs, so money was not a problem for me anymore. I was glad about it.

My first experience with getting high was scary because I did not know what to expect. My heart was beating fast as if I was having a heart attack. I broke out into a sweat that made me look as if I jumped into a pool in my clothes. I would feel as if I could run so fast that people would miss me if they blinked their eyes. I also felt as if I could fly beyond the clouds, and nobody could touch me. These feelings came over my body, and I could not control them. I felt safe, as if no one could hurt me anymore until I heard grandma calling for me. Grandma was so upset that I did not answer her, but I couldn't until I came down from the high. Grandma Mollie would curse me out using every hurtful word she could think of at the time.

When I was high off drugs, it would block out everything and everybody. I was fourteen years of age doing drugs, so I did not have to deal with problems I faced at home. I even got into selling drugs to support my habit for free. I did not sell it as much, but I sold enough to satisfy my craving. I got high alone because I did not trust anyone. I did not want anyone to know what I was doing, so I did not get into trouble with grandma.

I went through a lot from a child to a young teenager. I would have to make up stories about my life to seem as if I lived a good life, but I knew that was far from the truth. When I would expose a little of the truth to people, they would look at me crazy. They would even treat us differently. I would feel as if they wanted nothing to do with Scholar and me afterward. Some even used my truth against me when I thought I made a friend. People would make fun of me when they heard some of my stories, so I knew it was best to keep the truth to myself. They had no idea what I went through daily. I was grateful to wake up because I knew it could have been another way. Nothing in life is promised to anyone, especially life. Grandma Mollie was getting sicker, but she still managed to be evil and nasty. After calling me every name under the sun, I grew numb. I wish I had at least one good thing to say about grandma, but I don't. I'm just happy she did not kill Scholar and me. I'm sure she thought of it, so I knew God was with us each day.

I remember listening to the kids at school tell stories about their families and how much fun they would have. They would talk about trips they took and enjoying one another's time. That was what I desired for my family. All Scholar and I received was beatings and had to keep our mouths shut about it. So, I have no good things to say about my childhood. I am just finally telling it like it was.

Even after we got older, we thought grandma would start treating us a little better, but that was not the case. I finally got tired of it all and wanted to run away or take my life. In my heart, I didn't want to take my life because the pain wasn't for me. My sister and I were dealt a bad hand in life. I just had to get out of that house. It got to the point that I couldn't breathe! My nerves were so bad, and I needed help. Getting high off drugs was not helping after a while. It seemed as if the numbness the drugs produced wore off faster and faster each time. Using the drugs to cope was all I knew. I had no other outlet. Therefore, I decided just to run away. I asked my cousin to help me get some of my clothes out of the house because I did not want grandma to catch me. Although he tried to stay out of it, he helped as much as he could.

Claudine and Robert walked into the house as I was gathering my clothes and spotted us. The crazy thing was they began to help me also and did not tell grandma on me. Claudine asked me where I was going, and I told her Kim's house to call Uncle Alfonso. I asked Scholar to join me, but she was too scared to leave. She told me to go ahead without her and not to forget her. Scholar stayed on my mind, but I never looked back. After I called Uncle Alfonso, he picked me up right away from Kim's house.

When you think everything is going well, the devil starts to work. Claudine couldn't keep it a secret where I was staying. Grandma Mollie must have given her some money, and Claudine ratted me out. The next thing I knew, grandma showed up at Uncle Alfonso's house with the police to take me back home with her. Poor Aunt Danielle didn't know what to do, and Uncle Alfonso got upset, fussing at grandma. Uncle Alfonso told grandma I was not leaving his house because she was abusive to me and to get away from his home with drama. Grandma became angry and told the police to bring me out of the house. The officer told grandma they could not bring me out of the house since I was of age to decide where I wanted to go. They also told Grandma Mollie that she could go to court to get custody, but if I could prove she was abusive, she would not win the case. The police told grandma she could even face jail time if abuse were proven, so it would be in her best interest to leave. Grandma Mollie was so furious that she told me never to step foot in her house again, then she left. As grandma got into the car, she began yelling at Uncle Alfonso. She told them they were going to reap what they sowed, and something terrible would happen to them. Grandma Mollie and Aunt Mary practiced voodoo. They would take the hair or clothes of the person that did them wrong to place curses on them. Their friends never knew that about them either. Grandma and Aunt Mary would open the Bible, light tall red candles that had pictures of Jesus on them, and began chanting. Voodoo was big down south. Grandma would channel evil spirits into doing things on her behalf. It was sad but true. Grandma and the police finally left Uncle Alfonso's house.

I dropped my head in disappointment and just stood at the front door. What could I do? I was not going to fight her or curse her out. I was not going to disrespect her, although she put me through hell. She did so-call raise me, or whatever you want to call it. I was relieved that I did not have to go back to her house. Aunt Danielle and Uncle Alfonso treated me well, just as they did before. I felt I finally had a chance at life. I had a lot to learn as a young teenager going on fifteen then. All I knew was being confined to a bedroom all the time, living from place to place, and being abused.

I found out why my mother could not raise us. It was because her mother and sister, Aunt Marry, would fight her every chance they got. They put her out of the house multiple times, and she would have to beg them to open the door. That was going on before Scholar and I were born. Uncle Alfonso would share these stories with me so I could have some closure concerning my mother. It wasn't that she did not want us, grandma took her to court and told them she was an unfit mother and could not raise her kids. The court took sides with grandma, and my mom lost custody of us. My mom turned to alcohol after dealing with so much from my grandma and Aunt Mary. Uncle Alfonso said she never did drugs, though. I guess addiction was waiting for all of us because it has hit every generation so far. I still desired to know my mother. I just wanted to see if she was okay and maybe visit her if I could. I finally got the chance to meet my mother at the age of twenty-one. I was so excited, and I knew that was the closure I needed. I felt she was a missing piece of the puzzle in my life. I thanked God for the time I got to spend with her until she passed away.

As life took its lefts and rights, I was thirty-three years old when I gave up using drugs. I asked God to take it away from me because I was tired of everything that came along with it, and He did. It became too expensive to continue. I realized I just needed more and more to feel the first high I ever felt, and even then, it was not the same. The drugs started taking over my body in a negative way. I was always exhausted once the high wore off. I did not look like myself anymore, forgot things quickly, etc. I could go on and on. Anything that we place in our body that isn't naturally supposed to be there will deteriorate our bodies sooner than expected. Once I turned my addiction to drugs over to God, I felt free! It was crazy because I used the drugs to feel free, and I thought it worked initially, but it was just a trick in my mind. When the devil is involved, we will find lie after lie. I was told drugs were ok because it helps us, but that is a lie and truth is nowhere to be found.

I am now fifty-three years old. I have seven sons, five daughters, and five grandkids. I have been married for eight beautiful years. I am a homeowner, a best-selling author, a master chef, and head consultant with a million-dollar company. Why I'm sharing this? Because everything my grandmother and Aunt Mary said about my life was not the plans that God had for me. I'm loving and compassionate to others. I encourage those that don't know how to encourage themselves because I remember when I was there. I'm now the light of Jesus Christ for my family because God lives in me. I am a voice God is using to make a difference wherever He leads me. I am not ashamed to do the work God has assigned for me. I am an ordained Evangelist, a wonderful grandmother, a present mother, and a loving wife. My husband even stands by me through thick and thin and loves me to the moon and back.

See, when I was told I would never be anything, I

believed it. I heard it so much I could not see past it. The abuse told me I was nothing, and the pain was all I deserved. I was hurt and torn down in all areas of my life and needed healing. I was old-looking and exhausted all the time because the stress of life wore me down. The stress took over my life and put my beauty in a box. I felt I had no reason to smile and lost sight of who I was. I was a book full of blank pages hoping to be filled. Who would fill me with the things I needed?

God stepped into my life and revealed to me that I belonged to Him and that He would fill me with Himself. God showed me every day that He was love, and that was what I had been looking for all my life. Back then, when I wanted to take my life, I had no idea that my life was not mines to take. God placed purpose on my life just as He did for everyone else. So, if you feel as if you are living in vain, it's because you have not tapped into your God-given purpose yet.

Today I know who I am. I am a queen, royalty, righteous in God, made in God's image, an author, a speaker, a creator, and so much more. God has given me the power of love, forgiveness, and a sound mind. I am now a roaring lion that no longer gives up because I have God on my side. Yes, that's me. My strength comes from the Lord alone, so I don't have to worry or depend on man. I, Grenita Smith-Hall, stand tall with the help of God. I crossed over the bridges of troubled waters and now free like a bird in the sky. God made me like a diamond, bright and beautifully shaped perfectly. Nothing was placed out of order. I can't be stopped because my dark days are behind me now that I walk in the light of Jesus Christ.

So, for those of you that have a story to tell, do it! Your story could serve as healing to someone else's life. I pray my story will impact lives all over the world. I pray open doors of strength and courage to you all. The weight of the world shall fall off your shoulders as you write your story. It may sound a little crazy, but it's ok to forgive those that hurt you. Love them despite the situation. Forgiveness is not for them. It's to free you from the past. It helps you to release the anger and to smile again. Peace will be your portion. Remember, you are wonderfully made and created in God's image.

God's blessing to you all!